TABLE OF CONTENTS

Get ready to rock the kitchen as you begin your own double life—as a chef! With help from Miley (and Hannah), Jackson, and Robby Stewart, Lilly Truscott, and Oliver Oken, things will really start cookin'! In no time you'll be whipping up Smokin' Oken Chili-Mac Skillet, Miley's Mini Subs, and Lilly Likey Shortcakes. You can make a lot of these recipes by yourself, but it's always a good idea to follow Hannah's lead and bring along your manager—er, an adult—in case you need help. Once you get the hang of chopping, measuring, mixing, and mashing, your transformation into a kitchen superstar will be complete (and you don't even need a wig)!

Hannah Montana

Sweet NIBLETS

ROCKIN' FOOD FOR ANY MEAL

Meredith® Books
Des Moines, IA

HANNAH MONTANA

Based on the series created by Michael Poryes and Rich Correll & Barry O'Brien
Copyright © 2008 by Disney Enterprises, Inc.

Meredith Books
1716 Locust Street
Des Moines, IA 50309-3023
meredithbooks.com

Printed in China.
First Edition.
ISBN: 978-0-696-24119-2

Editor: Sheena Chihak, R.D.
Art Direction: Chad Jewell
Graphic Design and Support Illustration: Mada Design, Inc.

Rico knows a thing or two about ham, considering he is one. Try his hammy breakfast quesadilla to see for yourself—wahaha!

Each American eats almost 80 pounds of tomatoes every year! That will give you a lot of vitamins A and C.

THE BEST-OF-BOTH-WORLDS
BREAKFAST SANDWICHES

Utensils

- Table knife
- Measuring cups
- Measuring spoons
- Medium skillet
- Pancake turner
- Hot pads
- Cutting board
- Sharp knife
- Wire whisk
- Shallow bowl
- Small saucepan
- Wooden spoon

Ingredients

½	cup reduced-fat or regular peanut butter
8	½-inch-thick slices whole wheat or multigrain bread
2	tablespoons honey
2	medium bananas
2	eggs
½	cup milk
¼	teaspoon ground cinnamon
1	tablespoon butter or margarine
½	cup spreadable fruit or reduced-sugar jam (any flavor)

Directions

1 Use table knife to spread peanut butter on 4 slices of the bread. Use spoon to drizzle honey over the peanut butter. Save until Step 2.

2 Peel bananas and throw away peel. On the cutting board, use sharp knife to cut each banana in half lengthwise. Cut across each banana half to make slices. Put banana slices on each of the 4 peanut butter-spread bread slices. Put the remaining 4 bread slices on top to make 4 sandwiches.

3 Crack eggs into shallow bowl. Add milk and cinnamon. Use the whisk to beat eggs and milk together. Dip each sandwich into egg mixture, turning to coat both sides. Place sandwiches on baking sheet. Save until Step 4.

4 Put butter in skillet or on griddle. Put skillet on burner. Turn burner to medium heat. Melt the butter. When butter is melted, use the pancake turner to carefully transfer sandwiches from baking sheet to skillet or griddle. Cook about 2 minutes or until golden brown on bottoms. Use pancake turner to turn sandwiches over. Cook about 2 minutes more or until golden brown. Turn off burner. Use hot pads to remove skillet or griddle from heat. Place skillet or griddle on cooling rack.

5 While the sandwiches are cooking, put spreadable fruit in small saucepan. Put saucepan on burner. Turn burner to medium-low. Heat until spreadable fruit is melted, stirring often with wooden spoon. Turn off burner. Remove saucepan from heat.

6 To serve, use sharp knife to cut each warm sandwich in half. Drizzle melted spreadable fruit over sandwiches.

Makes 8 servings

Nutrition Facts per serving:
278 calories, 10 g total fat, 58 mg cholesterol, 253 mg sodium, 39 g carbohydrate, 3 g fiber, 10 g protein.

If you're in the mood for something sweet and salty, this skillet sandwich gives you both flavors in one!

FOOD FACT

If you're like most American kids, you'll eat 1,500 peanut butter sandwiches by the time you finish high school!

13

BANANA PANCAKES

Utensils

- Measuring cups
- Measuring spoons
- Hot pads
- Wire cooling rack
- Large bowl
- Wooden spoon
- Medium bowl
- Wire whisk
- Potato masher or fork
- Griddle or large, heavy skillet
- Pancake turner
- Serving plate
- Foil

Ingredients

- 1¾ cups packaged buttermilk pancake mix
- ¼ teaspoon ground cinnamon
- 2 eggs
- 2 ripe medium bananas
- 2 cups milk
- 3 tablespoons butter, melted, or cooking oil
- ⅓ cup finely chopped walnuts or pecans
  Shortening
  Chopped nuts and bananas, if you like

Directions

1 Put pancake mix and cinnamon in large bowl. Use wooden spoon to stir. Save until Step 3.

2 Crack eggs into medium bowl. Beat with wire whisk until mixed. Peel bananas and throw away peel. Add bananas to eggs. Use the potato masher or fork to mash bananas. Add the milk and melted butter to the banana mixture. Use whisk to beat until well mixed.

3 Add the banana mixture to the pancake mix mixture using wooden spoon to combine. (The batter will be somewhat lumpy.) Stir in the ⅓ cup nuts.

4 Lightly grease a griddle or large skillet with shortening. Put griddle or skillet on a burner. Turn heat to medium. (To check if the griddle or skillet is ready, carefully sprinkle a few drops of water on the surface. Water will dance across the surface when it is hot enough.)

5 For each pancake, pour about ¼ cup of the batter onto the hot griddle or skillet. Cook over medium heat until pancakes have slightly bubbly surfaces and the edges are slightly dry. (This will take 1 to 2 minutes.) Turn pancakes over with the pancake turner. Cook until bottoms are golden brown (1 to 2 minutes more). Remove pancakes and put them on a serving plate. Cover with foil to keep warm. Repeat until all of the batter is used. Turn off burner. Top with chopped nuts and/or bananas, if you like.

Makes 20 pancakes

Nutrition Facts per pancake:
94 calories, 4 g total fat, 28 mg cholesterol, 161 mg sodium, 11 g carbohydrate, 1 g fiber, 3 g protein.

CHOCOLATE PANCAKES

Utensils

- Measuring cups
- Measuring spoons
- Large bowl
- Wooden spoon
- Medium bowl
- Wire whisk
- Griddle or large, heavy skillet
- Pancake turner
- Serving plate
- Foil
- Hot pads

Ingredients

1	cup all-purpose flour
$\frac{2}{3}$	cup whole wheat flour
$\frac{1}{3}$	cup unsweetened cocoa powder
$\frac{1}{4}$	cup sugar
1	teaspoon baking soda
$\frac{1}{4}$	teaspoon salt
1	egg
$2\frac{1}{4}$	cups buttermilk
3	tablespoons cooking oil
	Shortening
	Chocolate shavings, if you like

Directions

1 Put all-purpose flour, whole wheat flour, cocoa powder, sugar, baking soda, and salt in large bowl. Stir with wooden spoon to mix. Save until Step 2.

2 Crack egg into medium bowl. Add buttermilk and oil. Use wire whisk to beat together. Add buttermilk mixture to flour mixture using wooden spoon to combine. (The batter will be somewhat lumpy.)

3 Lightly grease griddle or skillet with shortening. Put griddle or skillet on a burner. Turn heat to medium. (To check if griddle or skillet is ready, carefully sprinkle a few drops of water on the surface. Water will dance across the surface when it is hot enough.) Turn heat down to medium-low.

4 For each pancake, pour about ¼ cup of the batter onto the hot griddle or skillet. Cook over medium-low heat until pancakes have slightly bubbly surfaces and the edges are slightly dry. (This will take 2 to 3 minutes.) Turn pancakes over with the pancake turner. Cook until bottoms are golden brown (2 to 3 minutes more). Remove pancakes and put them on a serving plate. Cover with foil to keep warm. Repeat until all the batter is used. Turn off burner. Top pancakes with chocolate shavings, if you like.

Makes 16 pancakes

Nutrition Facts per pancake:
102 calories, 4 g total fat, 16 mg cholesterol, 156 mg sodium, 15 g carbohydrate, 1 g fiber, 3 g protein.

*NOTE: Because of the chocolate, these pancakes cook at a lower temperature.

HANNAHOLOGY

Robby adds vanilla and cinnamon to his pancakes to make them extra special.

STEWART FAMILY FRUIT-STUFFED PUFFS

Utensils

- Measuring cups
- Measuring spoons
- Four 4¼-inch pie plates or four 4½-inch foil tart pans
- Large bowl
- Wire whisk or rotary beater
- Baking sheet
- Custard cup or other small microwave-safe bowl
- Small spoon
- Hot pads
- Wire cooling rack
- Metal spatula
- 4 plates

Ingredients

Nonstick cooking spray

½ cup refrigerated or frozen egg product, thawed, or 1 whole egg plus 1 egg white

¼ cup all-purpose flour

¼ cup fat-free milk

1 tablespoon cooking oil

¼ teaspoon salt

2 tablespoons orange marmalade

2 cups fresh fruit (such as peeled and sliced kiwifruit, raspberries, blackberries, blueberries, sliced bananas, sliced strawberries, seedless grapes, peeled and sliced peaches, sliced nectarines, sliced apricots, and/or pitted and halved sweet cherries)*

2 tablespoons sliced almonds

Directions

1 Turn on oven to 400°. Lightly spray the pie plates or foil tart pans with cooking spray. Save until Step 3.

2 Put egg product, flour, milk, oil, and salt in large bowl. Beat together with wire whisk or rotary beater. Pour equal amounts of batter into each prepared pie plate or tart pan.

3 Pace pie plates or tart pans on baking sheet. Put baking sheet in oven. Bake about 25 minutes or until brown and puffy. Turn off oven. Let stand in oven for 5 minutes.

4 While the baked puffs are standing in the oven, spoon orange marmalade into custard cup. Place custard cup in microwave oven. Turn on microwave oven to 50% power (medium). Microwave for 30 seconds. Remove from microwave oven. Stir with small spoon. If marmalade is not melted, microwave about 10 seconds more.

5 Use hot pads to remove baking sheet from oven. Place baking sheet on cooling rack. Use metal spatula to quickly transfer puffs to 4 dessert plates.

6 Spoon some of the fruit into the center of each puff. Drizzle fruit with warmed orange marmalade. Sprinkle with sliced almonds. Serve at once.

Makes 4 servings

Nutrition Facts per serving:
159 calories, 5 g total fat, 0 mg cholesterol, 217 mg sodium, 24 g carbohydrate, 4 g fiber, 6 g protein.

*NOTE:
While the puffs are baking, peel and cut up the fruit.

16

Try these fluffy puffs to start your day the *Stewart* family way—a little nuts but well-balanced.

A game of tennis is a great way to get the whole family moving and having fun. Grab your racket and show your family that, just like Miley, you put the tennis in Tennessee!

MALIBU MORNING MUFFINS

Utensils

- Measuring cups
- Measuring spoons
- 2 muffin pans with 2½-inch cups
- 18 paper bake cups
- Large bowl
- Wooden spoon
- Vegetable peeler
- Apple corer/slicer
- Cutting board
- Sharp knife
- Medium bowl
- Wooden toothpick
- Hot pads
- Wire cooling racks

Ingredients

1	cup all-purpose flour
1	cup whole wheat flour
2	teaspoons baking soda
2	teaspoons ground cinnamon
½	teaspoon salt
1¼	cups packed brown sugar
2	medium apples
1¼	cups purchased finely shredded carrots
½	cup raisins
1	8-ounce can crushed pineapple (juice pack), undrained
⅔	cup cooking oil
3	eggs
½	teaspoon vanilla

Directions

1. Turn on oven to 375°. Line eighteen 2½-inch muffin cups with paper bake cups. Save until Step 5.

2. Put all-purpose flour, whole wheat flour, baking soda, cinnamon, and salt in large bowl. Stir with wooden spoon to combine. Stir in brown sugar. Save until Step 4.

3. Use the vegetable peeler to remove the peels from the apples. Discard the peels. Use apple corer/slicer to core and cut apples into wedges. On cutting board, use sharp knife to cut apple wedges into small pieces.

4. Add apples, carrots, and raisins to flour mixture. Stir with wooden spoon. Put undrained pineapple, oil, eggs, and vanilla into medium bowl. Stir with wooden spoon until well mixed. Add pineapple mixture to flour and apple mixture. Stir with wooden spoon just until dry ingredients are wet.

5. Spoon some of the batter into each muffin cup, putting equal amount in all cups.

6. Put muffin pans in oven. Bake about 18 minutes or until a wooden toothpick comes out clean. (To test for doneness, use hot pads to pull out oven rack. Stick toothpick in the center of one of the muffins; pull out toothpick. If any muffin sticks to it, carefully push the oven rack back into place using hot pads and bake the muffins a few minutes more; test again.) Turn off oven.

7. Use hot pads to remove muffin pans from the oven. Place muffin pans on cooling racks. Cool 5 minutes. Carefully remove muffins from muffin cups. Serve warm.

Makes 18 muffins

Nutrition Facts per muffin:
221 calories, 9 g total fat, 35 mg cholesterol, 227 mg sodium, 33 g carbohydrate, 2 g fiber, 3 g protein.

The beaches of Malibu and these delicious muffins both give you a taste of paradise, but for these muffins the only traveling you have to do is to the kitchen.

HANNAHOLOGY

Lilly's dad calls bran muffins "nature's broom."

19

GUARD-YOUR-BREAKFAST COOKIES

Utensils

- Measuring cups
- Medium bowl
- Fork
- Wooden spoon
- ¼-cup cookie scoop, if you like
- Large cookie sheet
- Rubber scraper, if necessary
- Hot pads
- Pancake turner
- Wire cooling rack
- Plastic wrap

Ingredients

1	egg
1	cup quick-cooking rolled oats
1	cup chunky peanut butter
½	cup sugar
½	cup raisins, dried cherries, or dried cranberries
⅓	cup unsweetened applesauce
¼	cup whole wheat flour
	Nonstick cooking spray

Directions

1 Turn on oven to 350°. Crack egg into medium bowl. Use fork to beat until mixed. Add oats, peanut butter, sugar, raisins, applesauce, and flour. Use wooden spoon to stir until combined.

2 Lightly spray ¼-cup cookie scoop or measuring cup with cooking spray. Scoop the dough with the scoop or measuring cup. Drop the dough onto an ungreased large cookie sheet using a rubber scraper, if necessary, to push the dough from the measuring cup. Fill the cookie sheet with mounds of dough, leaving about 3 inches between cookies. Use your clean hands to flatten each dough mound to a 3-inch round.

3 Put the cookie sheet in the oven. Bake about 14 minutes or until cookies are lightly browned.

4 Turn off oven. Use hot pads to remove cookie sheet from oven. Use the pancake turner to transfer cookies to the cooling rack. Let cookies cool on rack.

5 To store cookies, wrap each cookie in plastic wrap. Store at room temperature for up to 2 days or store in the freezer for up to 1 month. If cookies are frozen, thaw at room temperature before serving.

Makes about 10 cookies

Nutrition Facts per cookie:
262 calories, 14 g total fat, 21 mg cholesterol, 133 mg sodium, 30 g carbohydrate, 4 g fiber, 9 g protein.

Roxy's super sniffer would smell these delicious cookies from miles away. You might want to guard them so they don't disappear.

 FOOD FACT

The most popular usage of oatmeal, besides cereal, is in oatmeal cookies like these! Eating oats is a great way to get more fiber and other important minerals like zinc and magnesium.

POP STAR
BREAKFAST POCKETS

EGG-BACON POCKETS

Utensils

- Measuring cups
- Measuring spoons
- Cutting board
- Sharp knife
- Medium bowl
- Wire whisk or rotary beater
- Large nonstick skillet
- Spatula or wooden spoon
- Hot pads
- Wire coolling rack

Ingredients

2   large whole wheat or regular pita bread rounds

3   ounces Canadian-style bacon

1   cup refrigerated or frozen egg product, thawed

2   tablespoons sliced green onion, if you like

⅛   teaspoon salt

    Nonstick cooking spray

½   cup shredded reduced-fat cheddar cheese (2 ounces), if you like

Directions

1   On the cutting board, use the sharp knife to cut across each pita bread round to make 2 halves (4 halves total). Save until Step 4.

2   On cutting board, use the sharp knife to cut Canadian-style bacon into small pieces. Put bacon, egg product, green onion (if using), and salt in medium bowl. Use the wire whisk or rotary beater to beat until well mixed.

3   Lightly spray a nonstick skillet with cooking spray. Put skillet on burner. Turn burner to medium heat and heat skillet for 30 seconds. Pour egg mixture into hot skillet. Cook, without stirring, until mixture begins to set on the bottom and around edge. Using the spatula or wooden spoon, push the partially cooked egg mixture to the center, allowing uncooked mixture to flow to the edge of the skillet. Continue to cook about 2 minutes or until egg mixture is set but still glossy and moist. Turn off burner. Use the hot pads to remove skillet from burner at once. Place skillet on cooling rack.

4   Spoon egg mixture into pita bread halves. If you like, sprinkle with cheese. Serve at once.

Makes 4 servings

Nutrition Facts per serving:
141 calories, 2 g total fat, 10 mg cholesterol, 574 mg sodium, 19 g carbohydrate, 2 g fiber, 13 g protein.

The ham, broccoli, and cheese in these turnovers are hidden, just like Miley's secret identity.

Have you been hiding your jump-roping skills? Put on your favorite Hannah Montana song, jump rope to the beat, and see if, instead of a secret celebrity, you are a secret jump-roping star.

27

ROCKIN' PIZZA ROLLS

Utensils

- Measuring cup
- Baking sheet
- Pizza cutter or sharp knife
- Ruler
- Hot pads
- Spoon
- Pancake turner
- Wire cooling rack
- Plastic wrap

Ingredients

Nonstick cooking spray

Cornmeal, if you like

All-purpose flour

1   13.8-ounce package refrigerated pizza dough

1   3.5-ounce package pizza-style Canadian-style bacon (1½-inch diameter slices)

⅓   cup pizza sauce

3   1-ounce pieces string cheese, cut in half crosswise

Directions

1 Turn on oven to 400°. Lightly spray the baking sheet with cooking spray. If you like, lightly sprinkle cornmeal over the baking sheet. Save until Step 5.

2 Sprinkle a little flour on a flat work surface. Unroll pizza dough on floured surface. Use your fingers to press the dough to form a 13½×9-inch rectangle. Use pizza cutter or sharp knife to cut dough into six 4½-inch squares.

3 Put equal amounts of the Canadian-style bacon in the center of each square. Spoon some of the pizza sauce over Canadian-style bacon. Place the string cheese on top of the pizza sauce.

4 For each packet, use your fingers to grasp 2 opposite edges of the dough square and bring edges together. Pinch dough edges together to seal. Pinch the ends together to keep filling inside the packet.

5 Place the packets on the prepared baking sheet, placing them seam sides down. Put the baking sheet in the oven. Bake 13 to 18 minutes or until golden brown. Turn off oven.

6 Use hot pads to remove baking sheet from oven. Use pancake turner to remove pizza rolls from baking sheet to a cooling rack. Serve warm or cool completely.

Makes 6 pizza rolls

Nutrition Facts per pizza roll:
209 calories, 7 g total fat, 19 mg cholesterol, 524 mg sodium, 26 g carbohydrate, 1 g fiber, 10 g protein.

MAKE-AHEAD TIP:
Cool pizza rolls completely. Wrap each cooled pizza roll in plastic wrap. Chill in the refrigerator for at least 4 hours or up to 24 hours. If toting your lunch, pack wrapped pizza rolls in insulated containers with ice packs.

Unlike Jackson, these burritos don't need a weight machine: They are already beefed up and sure to impress.

Jackson lifts weights on his "rubber band" machine to keep his muscles strong. Strengthen your muscles by doing activities like lifting weights, shoveling snow, climbing a rope, or going hiking.

31

DOUBLE IDENTITY
CHICKEN SALAD

CHICKEN SALAD SANDWICHES

Utensils

- Measuring cups
- Measuring spoons
- Cutting board
- Sharp knife
- Medium bowl
- Wooden spoon
- Table knife

Ingredients

1	hard-cooked egg, chopped
1	cup chopped cooked chicken
⅓	cup chopped, cored apple, chopped seeded cucumber, or finely chopped celery
2	tablespoons plain low-fat yogurt
2	tablespoons light mayonnaise or salad dressing
	Salt
	Black pepper
8	slices whole wheat bread

Directions

1 Put the chopped egg, chicken, and apple in the medium bowl. Stir with wooden spoon. Add yogurt and mayonnaise. Stir with wooden spoon to mix. Sprinkle with salt and pepper. Stir with wooden spoon to mix.

2 Put the chicken mixture on 4 of the bread slices, putting equal amounts of chicken mixture on each slice. Use table knife to spread chicken mixture almost to edges of each bread slice.

3 Put the remaining 4 bread slices on top of chicken mixture to make 4 sandwiches. If you like, use the sharp knife to cut each sandwich into 4 triangles or squares.

Makes 4 sandwiches

Nutrition Facts per sandwich:
244 calories, 9 g total fat, 87 mg cholesterol, 432 mg sodium, 26 g carbohydrate, 4 g fiber, 17 g protein.

Pop stars and their friends aren't the only ones with alter egos. Here, chicken is served two ways: on a salad and in a sandwich.

COOL-AS-A CUCUMBER CHICKEN SALAD

Utensils

- Measuring cups
- Measuring spoons
- Kitchen scissors
- Large bowl
- Wooden spoon
- Screw-top jar
- 4 dinner plates

Ingredients

1	9-ounce package frozen chopped, cooked chicken or refrigerated cooked chicken, chopped
2	cups peeled, seeded, and cubed cantaloupe and/or halved seedless red grapes
1	cup chopped cucumber
⅓	cup orange juice
3	tablespoons salad oil
1	tablespoon snipped fresh mint or cilantro
	Salt
	Black pepper
4	cups packaged, torn mixed salad greens

Directions

1 Put chicken, cantaloupe, and cucumber in the large bowl. Stir with wooden spoon to mix. Save until Step 2.

2 To make the dressing, put orange juice, oil, mint or cilantro, a little salt, and a little pepper in the screw-top jar. Put lid on jar and close tightly. Shake until well mixed. Drizzle dressing over the chicken mixture. Use the wooden spoon to gently stir until chicken mixture is coated.

3 Put salad greens onto 4 dinner plates, putting equal amounts of greens on each plate. Spoon the chicken mixture onto the greens. Serve at once.

Makes 4 servings

Nutrition Facts per serving:
269 calories, 16 g total fat, 62 mg cholesterol, 114 mg sodium, 11 g carbohydrate, 1 g fiber, 22 g protein.

Lilly's double identity is Lola Luftnagle. Lola's hair is constantly changing colors. It could be white, purple, pink, blue, red, or whatever color Lola is in the mood for.

33

TURKEY AND BROCCOLI O'S

Utensils

- Measuring cups
- Cutting board
- Apple corer or sharp knife
- Sharp knife
- Toaster
- Small bowl
- Wooden spoon
- Plastic wrap, if you like

Ingredients

1	small green or red apple
4	whole grain bagels (buy split bagels)
1½	cups packaged shredded broccoli (broccoli slaw)
¼	cup reduced-fat honey-Dijon salad dressing
8	ounces deli-sliced roast turkey, roast beef, or ham
	More reduced-fat honey-Dijon salad dressing, if you like

Directions

1 On the cutting board, use the apple corer or sharp knife to remove the core from the apple. Use the sharp knife to cut the apple into thin rings. Save until Step 4.

2 Toast the bagel halves in the toaster until light brown.

3 Put the broccoli slaw and the ¼ cup salad dressing in small bowl. Stir with wooden spoon until broccoli is coated.

4 Put apple rings on bagel bottoms. Spoon broccoli mixture over apple rings. Put meat on top of broccoli mixture. Add bagel tops. If you like, wrap and chill in the refrigerator for up to 4 hours. If you like, serve with some more salad dressing for dipping.

Makes 4 sandwiches

Nutrition Facts per sandwich:
350 calories, 5 g total fat, 31 mg cholesterol, 873 mg sodium, 60 g carbohydrate, 7 g fiber, 18 g protein.

TIP:
For a vegetarian sandwich, replace the turkey with 4 slices of your favorite reduced-fat cheese.

Served on an O-shaped bagel, this sandwich is perfect for the Triple O. It might even get him a seat at the cafeteria's popular table.

 HANNAHOLOGY

Oliver, Lilly, and Miley usually eat lunch together in the Seaview High cafeteria.

MILEY'S MINI SUBS

Utensils

- Cutting board
- Sharp knife
- Small spoon
- Table knife

Ingredients

3   6-inch-long unsliced
     French-style rolls
     Yellow mustard
1   tomato
6   ounces thinly sliced
     cooked ham, roast beef,
     or cooked turkey
3   slices provolone, mozzarella,
     or Swiss cheese (3 ounces),
     halved
3   lettuce leaves

Directions

1 On the cutting board, use the sharp knife to carefully make a slit about 4 inches long on the top of each roll. Using the tip of the spoon, hollow out a ¾-inch-wide strip of bread along the slit. Use the table knife to spread the inside of each roll with mustard. Save until Step 3.

2 On the cutting board, use the sharp knife to cut the tomato into thin wedges.

3 Put some of the ham and a slice of cheese in each hollowed-out roll. Add a lettuce leaf and some of the tomato wedges to each sandwich. If you like, top with additional mustard. Cut the sandwiches in half.

Makes 6 servings

Nutrition Facts per serving:
155 calories, 7 g total fat, 26 mg cholesterol, 641 mg sodium, 12 g carbohydrate, 1 g fiber, 10 g protein.

Just like Miley, these sandwiches may be small, but they're sure to be a huge hit!

CENTER STAGE SALADS

CHEF ROBBY'S SALAD

Utensils

- Measuring cups
- Cutting board
- Sharp knife
- Egg slicer, if you like
- 4 large salad plates

Ingredients

4   ounces cooked lower-fat ham or turkey

8   cherry tomatoes

1   small yellow or red sweet pepper

6   cups packaged, torn mixed salad greens

½   cup shredded reduced-fat cheddar cheese (2 ounces)

1   hard-cooked egg, sliced

½   cup purchased croutons

½   cup bottled reduced-calorie ranch salad dressing

Directions

1 On the cutting board, use the sharp knife to cut the ham into short strips. Use the sharp knife to cut the cherry tomatoes in half. Save until Step 3.

2 Use the sharp knife to cut the yellow or red pepper in half from top to bottom. Pull off the stem and throw away. Remove seeds and soft white parts from inside pepper halves and throw away. Cut the pepper into short strips. Save until Step 3.

3 Put equal amounts of the salad greens onto the 4 salad plates. Put the ham strips, cheese, egg slices, tomato halves, and pepper strips on top of the greens. Sprinkle the croutons over the salads. Drizzle the salad dressing evenly over the salads.

Makes 4 servings

Nutrition Facts per serving:
191 calories, 11 g total fat, 85 mg cholesterol, 783 mg sodium, 11 g carbohydrate, 2 g fiber, 12 g protein.

These aren't any wimpy side salads. Loaded with toppings, they are the main event of your meal.

WIKI-WIKI WHEELIE HAM SALAD

Utensils

- Measuring cups
- Measuring spoons
- Cutting board
- Sharp knife
- Large saucepan
- Hot pads
- Colander
- Large bowl
- Wooden spoon
- Small bowl
- Plastic wrap

Ingredients

4	ounces dried wagon wheel pasta (1½ cups)
4	ounces cooked lean ham, chopped
1	small zucchini, chopped
2	tablespoons sliced green onion, if you like
⅓	cup bottled reduced-fat ranch salad dressing
2	tablespoons plain low-fat yogurt
1	teaspoon dried basil, crushed
¾	cup grape or cherry tomatoes

Directions

1 Cook wagon wheel pasta in the large saucepan following the package directions. Turn off the burner. Use hot pads to remove saucepan from burner. Place colander in sink. Carefully pour pasta into the colander. Run cold water over the pasta in colander. Stir pasta with wooden spoon. Run cold water over pasta again.

2 Put drained pasta, ham, and zucchini in the large bowl. If you like, add green onion. Stir with wooden spoon until combined.

3 To make dressing, put salad dressing, yogurt, and basil in the small bowl. Stir with wooden spoon until combined. Pour dressing over pasta mixture. Stir gently with wooden spoon until pasta is coated. Cover with plastic wrap. Chill in the refrigerator at least 2 hours or up to 24 hours.

4 To serve, on the cutting board, use sharp knife to cut each tomato in half. Add tomatoes to pasta and ham mixture. Stir gently with wooden spoon.

Makes 4 servings

Nutrition Facts per serving:
214 calories, 8 g total fat, 23 mg cholesterol, 596 mg sodium, 27 g carbohydrate, 2 g fiber, 10 g protein.

MOVIN' IT

Dancing on stage as Hannah Montana gives Miley a great workout. You may not have a sold-out audience to perform for, but you can put on your favorite song and dance in your room or perform for your friends and family.

39

BUCKY KENTUCKY CHICKEN STICKS

Utensils

- Baking sheet
- Foil
- Measuring cups
- Measuring spoons
- Wooden spoon
- 2 shallow dishes
- Hot pads
- Sharp knife
- Wire cooling rack
- Custard cup or other small microwave-safe bowl
- Waxed paper

Ingredients

1   cup fish-shape pizza-flavored, buffalo-wing-flavored, or colored crackers, crushed (about 2 ounces)

2   tablespoons fine dry bread crumbs

⅓   cup buttermilk

     14 to 16 ounces chicken breast tenderloins

¼–½ cup pizza sauce, bottled reduced-calorie ranch salad dressing, or bottled barbecue sauce

Directions

1 Turn on the oven to 400°. Line the baking sheet with foil. Save until Step 3.

2 Put cracker crumbs and bread crumbs in a shallow dish. Stir with wooden spoon. Pour buttermilk into the other shallow dish.

3 Using your clean fingers, pick up a chicken tenderloin and dip chicken in the buttermilk. Dip in the crumb mixture and turn to coat. Put on prepared baking sheet. Repeat until all the chicken is dipped and coated, placing chicken in a single layer on prepared baking sheet.

4 Put baking sheet in the oven. Bake 12 to 15 minutes or until no pink color is left in the center of the chicken and the crumb mixture is golden brown. (To check chicken for doneness, use hot pads to remove baking sheet from oven and cut into a chicken piece with a sharp knife.) Turn off oven. Use hot pads to remove baking sheet from oven and place on cooling rack.

5 While the chicken is baking, pour pizza sauce (if using) into custard cup. Cover custard cup with waxed paper. Place in microwave oven and cook on 100% power (high) for 30 to 40 seconds or until warm.

6 Serve hot chicken with warm pizza sauce, salad dressing, or barbecue sauce.

Makes 4 servings

Nutrition Facts per serving:
203 calories, 4 g total fat, 59 mg cholesterol, 244 mg sodium, 14 g carbohydrate, 1 g fiber, 26 g protein.

Rico is always looking for new menu items for the Surf Shop. These bean- and cheese-topped nachos are sure to be a best seller.

DON'T FRY POTATO WEDGES

Utensils

- Measuring cups
- Measuring spoons
- 15x10x1-inch baking pan
- Heavy-duty foil
- Pastry brush
- Vegetable brush
- Cutting board
- Sharp knife
- Large bowl
- Wooden spoon
- Hot pads
- Pancake turner

Ingredients

4	teaspoons olive oil
4	medium baking potatoes (1½ pounds total)
½	teaspoon salt
⅛–¼	teaspoon freshly ground black pepper
¼	cup grated Parmesan cheese

Directions

1 Turn on the oven to 450°. Line baking pan with heavy-duty foil. Use the pastry brush to coat foil with half of the olive oil. Save until Step 3.

2 Scrub baking potatoes with the vegetable brush, leaving peel on. On the cutting board, use sharp knife to cut potatoes lengthwise into ½-inch-thick wedges. Put wedges in the large bowl. Add the remaining olive oil. Using wooden spoon, toss to coat potato wedges with oil.

3 Sprinkle potato wedges with salt and pepper. Toss with the wooden spoon to coat. Place potato wedges in a single layer in foil-covered baking pan.

4 Put baking pan in oven. Bake 12 minutes. Use hot pads to remove baking pan from oven. Use a pancake turner to carefully turn potato wedges. Sprinkle with Parmesan cheese. Use hot pads to return baking pan to oven. Bake 10 to 12 minutes more or until potatoes are tender and golden brown. Turn off oven. Use hot pads to remove baking pan from oven. Serve potatoes at once.

Makes 6 servings

Nutrition Facts per serving:
105 calories, 4 g total fat, 3 mg cholesterol, 262 mg sodium, 14 g carbohydrate, 1 g fiber, 3 g protein.

After forgetting his sunscreen, Jackson gets fried by the sun during a volleyball game. Don't let your food face the same fate; bake your potatoes instead of frying them.

The fries you get at most fast food restaurants have more than 200 calories and 10 grams of fat. A serving of these fries has only 105 calories and 4 grams of fat.

MOVIE NIGHT MUNCH MIX

Utensils

- Measuring cups
- Medium bowl
- Wooden spoon
- Storage container with tight-fitting lid

Ingredients

2 cups cinnamon-flavor oat square cereal

⅔ cup original- or cinnamon-flavor crisp baked apple pieces

½ cup shelled lightly salted pistachio nuts or coarsely chopped, toasted pecans

¼ cup golden raisins

Directions

1 Put cereal, apple pieces, nuts, and raisins in medium bowl. Use wooden spoon to toss until mixed. Place mix in the container. Cover with lid; seal tightly. Store at room temperature for up to 1 week.

Makes 6 (½-cup) servings

Nutrition Facts per serving:
164 calories, 6 g total fat, 0 mg cholesterol, 94 mg sodium, 25 g carbohydrate, 3 g fiber, 5 g protein.

CHOCOLATE CRUNCH MIX:

Place 2 cups sweetened oat square cereal, 1 tablespoon unsweetened dark or regular cocoa powder, and 1 teaspoon powdered sugar in a medium bowl. Use wooden spoon to toss until cereal is coated.

Add ⅔ cup original-flavor crisp baked apple pieces, ½ cup dry-roasted peanuts, and ¼ cup dried cranberries or banana chips. Stir with wooden spoon.

Makes 6 (½-cup) servings

Nutrition Facts per serving:
178 calories, 7 g total fat, 0 mg cholesterol, 116 mg sodium, 27 g carbohydrate, 3 g fiber, 5 g protein.

This crunchy mix is the perfect snack for one of Miley and Lilly's movie nights. Put on your movie jammies, mix up a batch, and host your own movie night!

The next time you have friends over, host a hula hoop contest to see who can keep their hula hoop off the ground longest. If your friends are over for a movie night, let the winner of the contest choose the movie.

FRICK-A-FRICK-A-FRESH FRUIT SMOOTHIES

MELON-BERRY SMOOTHIES

Utensils

- Measuring cups
- Measuring spoons
- Electric blender
- 4 glasses
- Rubber scraper

Ingredients

1	cup frozen unsweetened whole strawberries
1	cup cut-up cantaloupe
⅓	cup orange juice
¼	cup fat-free milk
1	tablespoon honey
1	cup ice cubes

Directions

1 Put strawberries, cantaloupe, orange juice, milk, and honey in the blender. Cover blender with the lid and blend on high speed until mixture is smooth. Turn off blender.

2 Add ice cubes to the blender. Cover with lid and blend until smooth. Pour drink into glasses. Use the rubber scraper to get all of the drink out of the blender.

Makes 4 servings

Nutrition Facts per serving:
57 calories, 0 g total fat, 0 mg cholesterol, 15 mg sodium, 14 g carbohydrate, 1 g fiber, 1 g protein.

These slurp-worthy smoothies would definitely give Oliver something to rap about. The icy fruit drinks make a perfect beachside sipper.

BLUEBERRY SHAKES

Utensils

- Measuring cups
- Measuring spoons
- Electric blender
- 5 glasses
- Rubber scraper

Ingredients

3	6-ounce cartons plain low-fat yogurt
1	cup fresh or frozen blueberries
½	cup crushed ice
¼	cup sugar
¼	cup fat-free milk
¼	teaspoon almond extract

Directions

1 Put yogurt, blueberries, ice, sugar, milk, and almond extract in the blender.

2 Cover blender with lid and blend on high speed until mixture is smooth. Turn off blender. Pour into glasses. Use the rubber scraper to get all of the drink out of the blender. Serve at once.

Makes 5 (6-ounce) servings

Nutrition Facts per serving:
125 calories, 2 g total fat, 6 mg cholesterol, 77 mg sodium, 22 g carbohydrate, 1 g fiber, 6 g protein.

MOVIN' IT

Don't have an ocean nearby for surfing or running in the sand? Instead walk, jog, skate, or bike to nearby places such as school, a neighbor's house, or the park.

PUDDING LOLLIPOPS

Utensils

- Measuring cups
- Measuring spoons
- 2 medium bowls
- Wire whisk or rotary beater
- Sixteen 3-ounce paper or plastic drink cups
- Foil
- 13x9x2 inch baking pan
- Small sharp knife
- 16 wooden sticks

Ingredients

1   4-serving-size package sugar-free instant chocolate or chocolate fudge pudding mix

4   cups fat-free milk

1   4-serving-size package sugar-free instant banana cream, butterscotch, pistachio, vanilla, and or white chocolate pudding mix

Directions

1 Put the chocolate pudding mix into medium bowl. Add 2 cups of the milk. Use the wire whisk or rotary beater to beat pudding about 2 minutes or until well mixed. Spoon about 2 tablespoons of the pudding into each cup.* Cover each cup with foil. Put cups in the baking pan. Put baking pan in the freezer. Freeze 1 hour.

2 Put desired flavor pudding mix in another medium bowl. Add the remaining 2 cups milk. Use the wire whisk or rotary beater to beat the pudding about 2 minutes or until well mixed.

3 Remove the baking pan with pudding-filled cups from freezer; uncover. Spoon 2 tablespoons of the second flavor of pudding over frozen pudding in each cup. Cover each cup with foil. Use the sharp knife to make a small slit in center of foil over each cup. Slide wooden stick through the hole into the pudding mixture in each cup. Put the baking pan in the freezer. Freeze 4 to 6 hours or until pudding pops are firm.

4 To serve, remove desired number of pops from freezer. Let stand at room temperature 15 to 20 minutes. Remove foil. Tear paper cups away or remove pops from plastic cups.

Makes 16 pops

Nutrition Facts per pop:
36 calories, 0 g total fat, 1 mg cholesterol, 194 mg sodium, 7 g carbohydrate, 0 g fiber, 2 g protein.

*NOTE:
If you'd like, switch the order of the pudding in some of the cups. Start with the light-colored pudding and top with the chocolate. You can also add a third pudding flavor to make three layers.

After a day at the beach or skateboarding around Malibu, Lilly needs to chill out. These frozen pops are the perfect cool-down.

MANGO POPS

Utensils

- Measuring cups
- Measuring spoons
- Small saucepan
- Wooden spoon
- Hot pads
- Electric blender
- Eight 3-ounce paper or plastic drink cups or pop molds
- Rubber scraper
- 8x8x2- or 9x9x2-inch baking pan (if using drink cups)
- Foil
- Small sharp knife
- 8 wooden sticks

Ingredients

⅓ cup peach or apricot nectar

1 teaspoon unflavored gelatin

⅓ of a 26-ounce jar refrigerated mango slices or one 8-ounce can peach slices, drained

2 6-ounce cartons vanilla or peach fat-free yogurt

Directions

1 Put nectar and gelatin in small saucepan. Use wooden spoon to stir until combined. Let stand 5 minutes. Place saucepan on a burner. Turn burner to medium heat. Cook and stir with the wooden spoon until gelatin is dissolved. Turn off burner. Use hot pads to remove saucepan from burner. Carefully pour into the blender.

2 Add drained mango or peach slices and yogurt to the blender. Cover blender with lid and blend on high speed until smooth. Turn off blender.

3 Pour equal amounts of blended fruit mixture into the cups or pop molds. Use rubber scraper to get all the mixture out of the blender. Put cups in the baking pan. Cover each cup or mold with foil. Use the sharp knife to make a small slit in center of the foil on each cup or mold. Slide a wooden stick through the hole into the fruit mixture in each cup or mold. Put the baking pan or molds in the freezer. Freeze 4 to 6 hours or until firm.

4 To serve, remove desired number of pops from freezer. Remove foil. Tear paper cups away, or remove pops from plastic cups or pop molds.

Makes 8 pops

Nutrition Facts per pop:
65 calories, 0 g total fat, 0 mg cholesterol, 26 mg sodium, 15 g carbohydrate, 0 g fiber, 2 g protein.

Skateboarding and in-line skating are great ways to get movin'. Strap on your helmet, elbow pads, and knee pads, and race a friend to see who's fastest.

53

MIXED-UP MILK SHAKES

Utensils

- Measuring cup
- Electric blender
- 2 glasses
- Rubber scraper
- Cutting board
- Long sharp knife

Ingredients

1   pint light vanilla ice cream

¾   cup low-fat chocolate milk or low-fat strawberry milk

1   100-calorie peppermint wafer bar or peanut butter wafer bar

Directions

1 Put ice cream and milk in the blender. Cover with lid and blend on high speed until mixture is smooth, stopping to press mixture down, if needed. Turn off blender. Pour drink into 2 glasses. Use rubber scraper to get all of the drink out of the blender.

2 Place wafer bar on a cutting board. Use a long, sharp knife to cut bar in half lengthwise. Add 1 piece of wafer bar to each glass.

Makes 2 servings

Nutrition Facts per serving:
360 calories, 11 g total fat, 44 mg cholesterol, 175 mg sodium, 55 g carbohydrate, 1 g fiber, 11 g protein.

Jackson is known to get things mixed up, like the kitchen plumbing and his choice of cars, but he's sure to get these three-ingredient shakes right.

MOVIN' IT

Bounce on a pogo stick as long as you can. You don't need to try to break a world record like Jackson, but, if you want, you can have a competition with a friend to see who can go the longest without stopping.

55

CONCERT CONCESSION STAND
PRETZELS

Utensils

- Measuring spoons
- Large baking sheet
- Foil
- Ruler
- Pastry brush
- Small bowl
- Wooden spoon
- Hot pads
- Pancake turner
- Wire cooling rack
- Small saucepan
- Serving bowl

Ingredients

  Nonstick cooking spray
1 11-ounce package (12) refrigerated breadsticks
1 tablespoon milk
1 tablespoon grated Parmesan cheese
½ teaspoon dried Italian seasoning, crushed
⅛ teaspoon garlic powder
  Pizza or pasta sauce, if you like

Directions

1 Turn on oven to 375°. Line the baking sheet with foil. Coat foil with cooking spray. Unroll breadstick dough. Use your fingers to separate dough into 12 strips. Use your hands to roll each strip into a thin rope that is about 18 inches long. Shape each rope into a loop by crossing the ends. Bring the ends up over the loop and press into the other side of the loop, forming a pretzel shape.

2 Put the pretzels on foil-covered baking sheet, leaving 2 inches between pretzels. Use the pastry brush to lightly coat each pretzel with milk. Put Parmesan cheese, Italian seasoning, and garlic powder in the small bowl. Stir with the wooden spoon until well mixed. Sprinkle cheese mixture over pretzels.

3 Place baking sheet in oven. Bake about 15 minutes or until pretzels are golden brown. Turn off oven. Use hot pads to remove baking sheet from oven. Use the pancake turner to transfer pretzels to the cooling rack.

4 If you like, put pizza or pasta sauce in small saucepan. Put saucepan on a burner. Turn burner to medium-high heat. Heat pizza sauce until warm, stirring now and then with wooden spoon. Spoon pizza sauce into the serving bowl. Serve pretzels with warm pizza sauce for dipping.

Makes 12 pretzels

Nutrition Facts per pretzel:
77 calories, 1 g total fat, 0 mg cholesterol, 192 mg sodium, 13 g carbohydrate, 0 g fiber, 2 g protein.

Miley gets herself twisted up in tricky situations all the time. Although getting twisted up may not be good for Miley, these breadsticks are even better when twisted like a pretzel.

When Josh takes Miley on a date to a Hannah Montana concert, Miley uses the excuse that she's going to get a pretzel so she can get back on stage as Hannah.

SURF'S UP CITRUS SALAD

Utensils

- Measuring cups
- Measuring spoons
- Colander
- Can opener
- Medium bowl
- Wooden spoon
- Plastic wrap

Ingredients

1   8-ounce can pineapple chunks (juice-pack)

½   cup miniature marshmallows

½   cup light dairy sour cream

1   11-ounce can mandarin orange sections

1   tablespoon coconut, toasted

Directions

1 Put colander in the sink. If needed, use a can opener to open can of pineapple chunks. Put the pineapple chunks and liquid in the colander, and let the liquid drain into the sink. Put drained pineapple chunks, marshmallows, and sour cream in medium bowl. Use wooden spoon to stir until combined.

2 If needed, use a can opener to open can of mandarin orange sections. Pour orange sections and liquid into colander and let the liquid drain into the sink. Gently fold drained mandarin orange sections into pineapple mixture. Cover bowl with plastic wrap.

3 Place bowl in refrigerator. Chill salad at least 2 hours or up to 24 hours. To serve, sprinkle with coconut.

Makes 4 servings

Nutrition Facts per serving:
138 calories, 3 g total fat, 10 mg cholesterol, 33 mg sodium, 26 g carbohydrate, 1 g fiber, 3 g protein.

This entire entrée cooks in one pan, so even Oliver can impress people with this smokin' meal.

Multigrain pasta looks and tastes like regular pasta but has more protein and fiber, so you get more of the nutrients you need to stay strong and healthy!

ONE-IN-A-MILLION PIZZA

Utensils

- Measuring cups
- Measuring spoons
- Can opener
- Large saucepan
- Colander
- Hot pads
- 12-inch pizza pan (with sides)
- Large bowl
- Fork
- Wooden spoon
- Large skillet
- 2 wire cooling racks
- Pizza cutter or sharp knife

Ingredients

- 1   4½-ounce jar (drained weight) sliced mushrooms drained, if you like
- 1   14½-ounce can Italian-style stewed tomatoes, undrained
- 2   cups dried multigrain rotini pasta (5 ounces)
- 2   eggs
      Nonstick cooking spray
- 1   cup shredded reduced-fat 4-cheese pizza cheese (4 ounces)
- ½   cup fat-free milk
- ¾   cup chopped green sweet pepper and/or chopped zucchini
- ½   teaspoon dried Italian seasoning, crushed
- ½   of a 6-ounce package sliced turkey pepperoni
- 2   tablespoons grated Parmesan cheese

Directions

1 Cook pasta in the saucepan following the package directions. (To test pasta for doneness, remove 1 piece with the wooden spoon, let it cool slightly, and bite into it. The center will be soft, not chewy.) When pasta is cooked, turn off burner. Place colander in sink. Use hot pads to remove saucepan from burner. Carefully pour pasta into the colander and let liquid drain into sink. Rinse pasta with cold water and let drain again. Save until Step 3.

2 Turn on the oven to 350°. Lightly spray pizza pan with cooking spray.

3 To make pasta crust, crack eggs into the large bowl. Use fork to beat until mixed. Add ½ cup of the pizza cheese and the milk. Stir with the wooden spoon. Add pasta and stir until pasta is coated. Use the wooden spoon to evenly spread the pasta mixture onto prepared pizza pan. Put pizza pan in oven. Bake 20 minutes.

4 While crust is baking, coat a large skillet with cooking spray. Place on burner. Turn burner to medium heat. Heat skillet 30 seconds. Carefully add green pepper to hot skillet. Cook until tender but still slightly crunchy, stirring all the time with the wooden spoon. Add undrained tomatoes and Italian seasoning. Bring to boiling. Turn heat down to medium-low. Cook, uncovered, about 10 minutes or until all the liquid is gone, stirring now and then with wooden spoon. If you like, stir in mushrooms. Turn off burner. Use hot pads to remove skillet from burner. Place on cooling rack.

5 Use hot pads to remove pizza pan from oven. Place on another cooling rack. Put pepperoni slices on pasta crust. Use wooden spoon to spoon tomato mixture over pepperoni. Sprinkle with the remaining ½ cup pizza cheese and the Parmesan cheese. Use hot pads to return pizza pan to oven. Bake 10 to 12 minutes more or until pizza is heated through and cheese is melted. Turn off oven.

6 Use hot pads to remove pizza pan from oven. Place on cooling rack. To serve, use a pizza cutter or sharp knife to cut pizza into 6 wedges.

Makes 6 servings

Nutrition Facts per serving:
239 calories, 7 g total fat, 100 mg cholesterol, 614 mg sodium, 26 g carbohydrate, 2 g fiber, 17 g protein.

The chance that Miley would become a huge pop star was "One in a Million" and so is the chance that you've ever had a pizza like this one!

FOOD FACT

If you like your peppers extra sweet, choose red sweet peppers. Sweet peppers change color while they grow from green to yellow to red and keep getting sweeter as they grow.

JACKSANNAH SWEET-AND-SOUR CHICKEN

Utensils

- Measuring cups
- Measuring spoons
- Vegetable peeler
- Can opener
- Strainer
- 2 small bowls
- Wooden spoon
- Cutting board
- Sharp knife
- 2 medium bowls
- Large skillet
- Slotted spoon
- Plate
- Hot pads
- Wire cooling rack

Ingredients

1	medium red sweet pepper, thinly sliced
1	medium carrot, thinly sliced (about ½ cup)
1	8-ounce can pineapple chunks (juice-pack)
½	cup bottled sweet-and-sour sauce
12	ounces skinless, boneless chicken breasts
1	tablespoon reduced-sodium soy sauce
4	teaspoons cooking oil
1	cup fresh pea pods, tips and stems removed
2	cups hot cooked white or brown rice

Directions

1 Place a strainer in a small bowl. Pour pineapple and liquid into strainer. Let liquid drain into bowl. Put 2 tablespoons of the pineapple juice into another small bowl. Throw away the rest of the pineapple juice. Save pineapple until Step 5.

2 Use the wooden spoon to stir the sweet-and-sour sauce into the 2 tablespoons pineapple juice. Save until Step 5.

3 On the cutting board, use sharp knife to cut chicken into 1-inch pieces. Put chicken pieces in a medium bowl. Add soy sauce to chicken. Toss with wooden spoon until coated. Save until Step 5.

4 Put 3 teaspoons of the cooking oil into the skillet. Put the skillet on a burner. Turn burner to medium-high heat. Heat oil. (To tell when the oil is hot enough, sprinkle a couple of drops of water into the skillet. When the water drops dance on the surface, the oil is hot.) Add red pepper and carrot to hot oil. Cook for 3 minutes, stirring vegetables all the time with the wooden spoon. Add pea pods. Cook about 1 minute more or until the vegetables are tender but still slightly crunchy, stirring all the time with the wooden spoon. Use a slotted spoon to remove vegetables from the skillet to a plate.

5 Add the remaining 1 teaspoon oil to the skillet. Add chicken to skillet. Cook over medium-high heat for 3 to 4 minutes or until chicken is no longer pink, stirring chicken all the time with the wooden spoon. Add sweet-and-sour sauce mixture, vegetable mixture, and pineapple chunks to skillet. Cook until everything is hot. Turn off burner. Use hot pads to remove skillet from burner. Place skillet on cooling rack. Serve chicken mixture with hot cooked rice.

Makes 4 or 5 servings

Nutrition Facts per serving:
337 calories, 6 g total fat, 49 mg cholesterol, 297 mg sodium, 46 g carbohydrate, 3 g fiber, 23 g protein.

Just like this saucy dish, when you pair up these siblings, you get a combination that's a little sweet and a little sour.

When the paparazzi follow Hannah home, Jackson has to pretend to be Hannah Montana's boyfriend so her cover isn't blown.

NO-TRICKS FISH STICKS, YOU CAN FIX, JUST FOR KICKS

Utensils

- Measuring cups
- Measuring spoons
- 2-quart square or rectangular baking dish
- Can opener
- Large spoon
- Hot pads
- Wire cooling rack

Ingredients

1   11-ounce package (18) frozen baked, breaded fish sticks
1   8-ounce can pizza sauce
1   cup shredded mozzarella cheese (4 ounces)
2   tablespoons shredded fresh basil, if you like

Directions

1 Turn on the oven to 425°. Put fish sticks in baking dish. Sprinkle with mozzarella cheese.

2 Put baking dish in oven. Bake about 20 minutes or until fish sticks are heated through. Turn off oven. Use hot pads to remove baking dish from oven. Place baking dish on cooling rack. If you like, sprinkle fish sticks with basil. Serve with warm pizza sauce.

Makes 4 servings

Nutrition Facts per serving:
231 calories, 8 g total fat, 37 mg cholesterol, 728 mg sodium, 23 g carbohydrate, 0 g fiber, 16 g protein.

By the time she's finished, Lilly's rhymes can start sounding fishy. This rhyming recipe for seasoned fish sticks is perfect for her.

When Miley asks Lilly if Amber is going to be hurt by their prank, Lilly responds with a rhyme: "Just her pride, nationwide, nowhere to hide, humilified, sad inside."

ITALIAN FOOD LOVERS SAY WHAT?

Utensils

- Measuring cups
- Measuring spoons
- Kitchen scissors
- Cutting board
- Sharp knife
- Can opener
- Colander
- 2 large saucepans
- Wooden spoon
- Hot pads
- Wire cooling rack

Ingredients

1	large onion, finely choppped
1	medium green, red, or yellow sweet pepper, finely chopped
1	14½-ounce can diced tomatoes, undrained
1	8-ounce can tomato sauce
1	4-ounce can (drained weight) sliced mushrooms
	Nonstick cooking spray
1	teaspoon bottled minced garlic
½	cup chopped, thinly sliced cooked turkey pepperoni
1	tablespoon snipped fresh oregano or basil or 1 teaspoon dried oregano or basil, crushed
⅛-¼	teaspoon crushed red pepper, if you like
8-10	ounces dried whole grain pasta
⅓	cup shredded Parmesan cheese
	Fresh oregano sprigs, if you like

Directions

1 Use the can opener to open the cans of diced tomatoes, tomato sauce, and mushrooms. Place the colander in sink. Pour mushrooms and liquid into colander and let liquid drain into the sink. Save until Step 3.

2 Spray a large saucepan with cooking spray. Put saucepan on burner. Turn burner to medium heat and heat saucepan for 30 seconds. Carefully add onion, green pepper, and garlic to hot saucepan. Cook vegetables until tender, stirring now and then with wooden spoon.

3 Add undrained tomatoes, tomato sauce, and mushrooms. Stir with the wooden spoon. Add pepperoni, dried oregano (if using) and, if you like, crushed red pepper. Bring to boiling. Turn heat down to medium-low. Cook, uncovered, about 10 minutes or until desired consistency, stirring now and then with wooden spoon. Turn off burner. Use hot pads to remove saucepan from burner. Place on cooling rack.

4 Meanwhile, cook pasta in another large saucepan following the package directions. (To test pasta for doneness, remove a piece with the wooden spoon, let it cool slightly, and bite into it. The center will be soft, not chewy.) When pasta is cooked, turn off burner. Place colander in sink. Use hot pads to remove saucepan from burner. Carefully pour pasta into the colander and let liquid drain into sink.

5 If using snipped fresh oregano, stir into tomato mixture just before serving. Serve tomato mixture over hot cooked pasta. Sprinkle each serving with Parmesan cheese. If you like, add a fresh oregano sprig to each serving.

Makes 6 to 8 servings

Nutrition Facts per serving:
224 calories, 4 g total fat, 21 mg cholesterol, 670 mg sodium, 38 g carbohydrate, 2 g fiber, 13 g protein.

That's right, with a pizza-flavored sauce, this delicious dish gives you a taste of two Italian classics—pizza and pasta!

MOVIN' IT

Soccer is a popular sport in Italy that is a lot of fun to play with friends. If your friends can't play, practice dribbling the ball or other cool soccer tricks on your own!

TOP-THE-CHARTS TORTELLINI SALAD

Utensils

- Measuring cups
- Cutting board
- Sharp knife
- Large saucepan
- Wooden spoon
- Colander
- Hot pads
- Large bowl

Ingredients

1 7- to 8-ounce package dried cheese-filled tortellini

8 cherry tomatoes, quartered

1 cup chopped, cooked smoked turkey, ham, or chicken

½ cup coarsely chopped green sweet pepper

¼ cup sliced, pitted ripe olives, if you like

¼ cup bottled Italian vinaigrette or balsamic vinaigrette salad dressing

Black pepper

Directions

1 Cook tortellini in the saucepan following package directions. (To test tortellini for doneness, remove 1 piece with the wooden spoon, let it cool slightly, and bite into it. The center will be soft, not chewy.) When tortellini is cooked, turn off burner. Place colander in sink. Use hot pads to remove saucepan from burner. Carefully pour tortellini into the colander and let liquid drain into sink. Rinse tortellini with cold water; drain again.

2 Put tortellini, tomatoes, turkey, green pepper, and, if you like, olives in large bowl. Drizzle salad dressing over mixture. Toss with the wooden spoon until tortellini is coated. Sprinkle with black pepper. Serve at once.

Makes 4 servings

Nutrition Facts per serving:
330 calories, 15 g total fat, 20 mg cholesterol, 897 mg sodium, 32 g carbohydrate, 1 g fiber, 17 g protein.

TIP:
For a vegetarian salad, replace the turkey with 1 cup chopped raw broccoli or cauliflower.

After this dish debuts at the dinner table, it will quickly climb to No. 1!

Set up an obstacle course in your yard and have somebody time you going through it. Each time through, try to break your record.

ROXY'S BURGER REMEDY

Utensils

- Measuring cups
- Measuring spoons
- Large bowl
- Waxed paper
- Ruler
- Broiler pan
- Pastry brush
- Hot pads
- Pancake turner
- Wire cooling rack

Ingredients

1	pound ground beef
¼	cup bottled honey-barbecue sauce
¼	teaspoon salt
¼	teaspoon black pepper
4	fresh or canned pineapple slices
2	cups prewashed fresh spinach leaves or 4 leaf lettuce leaves or romaine leaves
4	whole wheat hamburger buns, split and toasted
	Bottled honey-barbecue sauce, if you like

Directions

1 Turn on broiler. Put ground beef, 2 tablespoons of the barbecue sauce, the salt, and pepper in a large bowl. Use your hands to mix well. Place a piece of waxed paper on the counter or table. Put ground beef mixture on waxed paper. Use your hands to divide meat into 4 equal portions. Shape each portion into a flat, round patty that measures about ½-inch thick. Place patties on the rack of the broiler pan. Wash your hands well using soap and warm water. Place broiler pan in broiler.* Broil 6 minutes.

2 While the patties are broiling, use the pastry brush to brush all sides of the pineapple slices with the remaining 2 tablespoons barbecue sauce. Use hot pads to pull broiler rack out from broiler. Put pineapple slices next to beef patties. Use a pancake turner to turn patties. Use hot pads to push broiler rack back into broiler. Broil about 6 minutes more or until patties are done (160°F)** and pineapple is hot, turning pineapple once using the pancake turner. Turn off broiler. Use hot pads to remove broiler pan from broiler. Place on a cooling rack.

3 To serve, place spinach leaves on bun bottoms. Top each bun bottom with a beef patty and a pineapple slice. If you like, drizzle the pineapple with more barbecue sauce. Add bun tops.

Makes 4 servings

Nutrition Facts per serving:
380 calories, 19 g total fat, 77 mg cholesterol, 563 mg sodium, 29 g carbohydrate, 3 g fiber, 24 g protein.

TIP:
To toast hamburger buns, turn on broiler. Put bun halves, cut sides up, on the unheated rack of a broiler pan. Put broiler pan in broiler. Broil about 5 minutes or until buns are lightly toasted, checking every minute to make sure buns do not get too brown. Turn off broiler. Use hot pads to remove broiler pan from broiler. Place on wire cooling rack.

*NOTE:
Be extra careful when broiling not to get burned. Have an adult help you to be safe.

**NOTE:
Patties are done when the centers reach 160°F. Ask an adult to help you check the temperature with an instant-read thermometer.

Roxy has a lot of strange home remedies, but this one actually works! This saucy sandwich is the remedy for boring burgers.

HANNAHOLOGY

Roxy was the one who picked out the Hannah wig to complete Miley's disguise for her double identity.

SOUPERSTAR BOWLS

TEXAS CHILI MADE EASY

Utensils

- Measuring cups
- Measuring spoons
- Can opener
- Large skillet with lid
- Wooden spoon
- Colander
- Medium bowl
- Hot pads
- Wire cooling rack
- Disposable container

Ingredients

1	15-ounce can pinto beans, undrained
12	ounces lean ground beef
1	cup bottled salsa
½	cup beef broth
1	teaspoon chili powder
½	teaspoon ground cumin
	Sour cream, if you like

Directions

1 Use can opener to open can of pinto beans. Save for Step 3.

2 Put ground beef in the large skillet. Put the skillet on burner. Turn burner to medium-high heat. Break up meat with the wooden spoon. Cook until no pink color is left in the meat, stirring now and then with the wooden spoon. This will take 8 to 10 minutes. Put colander over the bowl. Turn off burner. Use hot pads to remove skillet from burner. Place on cooling rack. Spoon meat and juices into the colander and let the fat drain into the bowl. Spoon meat back into skillet. Put cooled fat in a container and throw away.

3 Stir undrained beans, salsa, beef broth, chili powder, and cumin into meat in skillet. Put skillet on burner. Turn burner to medium-high heat. Bring to boiling. Turn down heat to low. Cover skillet with lid. Cook about 10 minutes or until everything is hot. Turn off burner. Use hot pads to remove skillet from burner and place on cooling rack. If you like, serve with sour cream.

Makes 6 servings

Nutrition facts per serving:
178 calories, 8 g total fat, 36 mg cholesterol, 442 mg sodium, 12 g carbohydrate, 4 g fiber, 15 g protein.

TURKEY NOODLE SOUP

Utensils

- Measuring cups
- Measuring spoons
- Kitchen scissors
- Vegetable peeler
- Cutting board
- Sharp knife
- Large saucepan with lid
- Wooden spoon
- Hot pads

Ingredients

2	medium carrots
1	stalk celery
1	medium onion
1	medium yellow summer squash
3	cups reduced-sodium chicken broth
2¼	cups water
1½	cups chopped cooked turkey or chicken
2	teaspoons snipped fresh thyme or 1 teaspoon dried thyme, crushed
2	cups dried wide noodles
2	tablespoons lemon juice

Directions

1 Use the vegetable peeler to peel carrots. On the cutting board, use sharp knife to cut the ends off the carrots and celery. Throw away the peel and ends. Use the sharp knife to cut the carrots and celery into thin slices. Use the sharp knife to cut the onion into thin wedges. Save until Step 2. Use the sharp knife to cut squash lengthwise into 4 long pieces and then cut across pieces into slices. Save until Step 3.

2 Put carrots, celery, onion, chicken broth, the water, the turkey, and, if using, dried thyme in large saucepan. Put saucepan on burner. Turn burner to medium-high heat. Bring to boiling. Turn down heat to medium-low. Cover saucepan with lid. Cook 15 minutes, stirring now and then with the wooden spoon.

3 Use hot pads to carefully remove lid from saucepan. Use wooden spoon to stir in squash and uncooked noodles. Cook, uncovered, 10 to 12 minutes or until the noodles are tender. (To test noodles for doneness, remove 1 noodle with the wooden spoon, let it cool slightly, and bite into it. The center will be soft, not chewy.) Stir in lemon juice and, if using, fresh thyme. Cook, uncovered, 1 minute more.

Makes 5 servings

Nutrition Facts per serving:
163 calories, 3 g total fat, 46 mg cholesterol, 424 mg sodium, 17 g carbohydrate, 2 g fiber, 17 g protein.

FOOD FACT

Red beans, like pinto beans, are nutritional superfoods! They are loaded with protein, fiber, copper, iron, and much more.

SWEET NIBLETS

If your dinner guests are calling for an encore, offer them a sweet ending with one of these delicious desserts. These recipes are lower in sugar but so tasty that even Jackson's sweet tooth would be satisfied. When you get to enjoy dessert without all the sugar, it's "The Best of Both Worlds"!

Filled with fruit, cream cheese, and yogurt, this delicious dessert is Lilly's perfect way to end a meal.

MOVIN' IT

Lilly has some impressive gymnastics skills. You may not be able to do all the stunts she can, but you still can get a workout by doing simple moves like somersaults and cartwheels.

83

CHOCOLATE-STRAWBERRY PARFAITS

Utensils

- Measuring cups
- Cutting board
- 2 sharp knives
- 4 parfait glasses or dessert dishes
- Large spoon

Ingredients

8   reduced-fat graham cracker squares
2   cups fresh strawberries
1   ounce dark chocolate
1   cup vanilla low-fat yogurt
    Fresh mint leaves, if you like

Directions

1 Use your fingers to break graham cracker squares into bite-size pieces. Save until Step 2. On the cutting board, use sharp knife to remove the green tops from the strawberries and halve or quarter each strawberry. Save until Step 2. Use another sharp knife to cut the chocolate into small pieces. Save until Step 3.

2 Place half of the graham cracker pieces in 4 parfait glasses or dessert dishes. Top with half of the strawberries. Spoon half of the yogurt over strawberries. Repeat layers.

3 Sprinkle some of the chopped chocolate over each parfait. If you like, add a fresh mint leaf to each parfait.

Makes 4 servings

Nutrition Facts per serving:
141 calories, 3 g total fat, 3 mg cholesterol, 87 mg sodium, 24 g carbohydrate, 2 g fiber, 4 g protein.

Robby likes impressing people with his skills in the kitchen. With multiple layers, these parfaits may look like they take skills, but they're really a snap!

BLUEBERRY-CARAMEL CHEESECAKE PARFAITS

Utensils

- Measuring cups
- Medium bowl
- Wire whisk or rotary beater
- Plastic wrap
- Rubber scraper
- Resealable plastic bag
- Rolling pin
- Large spoon
- 4 parfait glasses or dessert dishes

Ingredients

1   4-serving-size package fat-free, sugar-free, reduced-calorie cheesecake-flavored instant pudding mix

2   cups fat-free milk

¼   cup caramel ice cream topping

2   100-calorie packets shortbread cookies

1½   cups fresh blueberries

Directions

1 Put pudding mix in medium bowl. Add milk. Use the wire whisk or rotary beater to beat the pudding about 2 minutes or until well mixed. Cover bowl with plastic wrap. Place in refrigerator. Chill until starting to set (about 10 minutes). Use rubber scraper to fold in caramel ice cream topping.

2 Put cookies in a resealable plastic bag. Seal bag. Use the rolling pin to roll over the cookies, coarsely crushing them.

3 Spoon half of the pudding mixture into 4 parfait glasses or dessert dishes. Top each with some of the blueberries. Top with the remaining pudding mixture. Sprinkle with crushed cookies.

4 Cover each glass or dish with plastic wrap. Place in the refrigerator. Chill up to 24 hours.

Makes 4 servings

Nutrition Facts per serving:
199 calories, 2 g total fat, 3 mg cholesterol, 479 mg sodium, 42 g carbohydrate, 2 g fiber, 5 g protein.

FOOD FACT

Blueberries make almost everyone's list of superfoods because they are jam-packed with vitamins and minerals like vitamins C and K and manganese. Plus they are low in calories and high in fiber!

85

WHAT-YOU-MAKE-IT BROWNIES

Utensils

- Measuring cups
- Measuring spoons
- 12-inch pizza pan (with sides)
- Cutting board
- Table knife
- Medium bowl
- Electric mixer
- Rubber scraper
- Hot pads
- Wire cooling rack
- Sharp knife
- 12 dessert plates

Ingredients

Nonstick cooking spray
3   tablespoons butter
½   cup sugar
¼   cup refrigerated or frozen egg product, thawed
¾   cup chocolate-flavored syrup
⅔   cup all-purpose flour
3   cups assorted fruit (such as sliced, peeled kiwifruits; mandarin orange sections; sliced bananas; sliced, peeled peaches; sliced nectarines; strawberries; raspberries; and/or blueberries)
½   cup chocolate-flavored syrup

Directions

1 Turn on oven to 350°. Lightly coat pizza pan with cooking spray. Set aside.

2 To make crust, on the cutting board, use a table knife to cut butter into pieces. Place butter in medium bowl. Beat with an electric mixer on medium speed about 30 seconds or until butter is softened. Stop the mixer. Add sugar. Beat on medium speed until creamy. Stop the mixer. Add the egg; beat on medium speed until well mixed. Stop the mixer.

3 Add one-third of the ¾ cup chocolate-flavored syrup; beat on low speed until combined. Add one-third of the flour; beat on low speed until combined. Repeat until all of the ¾ cup chocolate-flavored syrup and flour are used. Use rubber scraper to spread batter evenly onto the prepared pizza pan.

4 Put pizza pan in the oven. Bake about 20 minutes or until the top of the brownies springs back when you lightly touch it. Turn off oven. Use hot pads to remove pizza pan from the oven. Place on the cooling rack; cool.

5 To serve, use a sharp knife to cut the pan of brownies into 12 wedges. Top wedges with fruit. Drizzle with the ½ cup chocolate-flavored syrup.

Makes 12 servings

Nutrition Facts per serving:
187 calories, 3 g total fat, 8 mg cholesterol, 61 mg sodium, 39 g carbohydrate, 2 g fiber, 2 g protein.

As Hannah would say, "Life's What You Make It," and so are these brownies when you choose your favorite fruit toppings.

Kiwifruits are sometimes called Chinese gooseberries. No matter what you call them, they always provide your body with vitamin C and fiber.

NUTS-ABOUT-OATMEAL COOKIES

Utensils

- Measuring cups
- Measuring spoons
- Table knife
- Large bowl
- Electric mixer
- Rubber scraper
- Wooden spoon
- Teaspoon
- Cookie sheet
- Hot pads
- Wire cooling rack
- Pancake turner

Ingredients

½	cup butter
½	cup reduced-fat peanut butter
⅓	cup granulated sugar
⅓	cup packed brown sugar
½	teaspoon baking soda
1	egg
½	teaspoon vanilla
1	cup all-purpose flour
1	cup quick-cooking rolled oats

Directions

1 Turn on the oven to 375°. Use table knife to cut butter into pieces. Put butter in a large bowl. Beat with electric mixer on medium speed about 30 seconds or until butter is softened. Stop the mixer. Add peanut butter. Beat on medium speed until combined, stopping the mixer now and then and using rubber scraper to scrape the side of the bowl. Stop the mixer.

2 Add granulated sugar, brown sugar, and baking soda to peanut butter mixture. Beat on medium speed until combined, stopping the mixer now and then and scraping the side of the bowl with the rubber scraper. Stop the mixer. Add the egg and vanilla. Beat on medium speed until combined. Beatin as much of the flour as you can with the mixer. Use wooden spoon to stir in any remaining flour. Stir in oats.

3 Use a teaspoon to drop the dough by rounded teaspoons onto ungreased cookie sheet, leaving 2 inches between cookies.

4 Put cookie sheet in the oven. Bake 7 to 8 minutes or until edges of cookies are golden brown. Use hot pads to remove cookie sheet from the oven. Place on cooling rack. Cool cookies on cookie sheet 1 minute. Use a pancake turner to transfer cookies from cookie sheet to cooling rack. Repeat with remaining dough, letting cookie sheet cool between batches or using a second cookie sheet. Turn off oven.

Makes about 40 cookies

Nutrition Facts per cookie:
73 calories, 4 g total fat, 11 mg cholesterol, 54 mg sodium, 9 g carbohydrate, 1 g fiber, 2 g protein.

Miley was nuts about Jake. Oliver was nuts about Hannah. Lilly was nuts about Luke. And Jackson is just nuts! But everyone will be nuts about these cookies!

MINI MONKEY BREAD

Utensils

- Measuring cups
- Measuring spoons
- Hot pads
- Muffin pan with twelve 2½-inch cups
- Kitchen scissors
- Ruler
- Small bowl
- Wire whisk
- Wire cooling rack
- Large serving plate

Ingredients

Nonstick cooking spray
1   1-pound loaf frozen whole wheat bread dough, thawed
½   cup raisins or mixed dried fruit bits
½   cup chopped pecans, if you like
3   tablespoons butter, melted
¼   cup honey
1   teaspoon ground cinnamon

Directions

1 Turn on oven to 350°. Generously coat twelve 2½-inch muffin cups with cooking spray.

2 Use kitchen scissors to snip bread dough into 1-inch pieces. Put half of the dough pieces in the prepared muffin cups. Top with raisins. If you like, sprinkle with pecans. Place remaining dough pieces on top of the raisins and pecans.

3 Put the melted butter, honey, and cinnamon in the small bowl. Use wire whisk to beat until combined. Drizzle mixture evenly over dough in muffin cups.

4 Put pan in oven. Bake 16 to 18 minutes or until bread is golden brown. Use hot pads to remove pan from oven. Place pan on cooling rack and cool 3 minutes. Place the large serving plate on top of the pan. Using hot pads, turn plate and pan over so plate is on the bottom. Set on countertop. Carefully lift off pan. Cool slightly. Serve warm.

Makes 12 servings

Nutrition Facts per serving:
163 calories, 4 g total fat, 8 mg cholesterol, 231 mg sodium, 29 g carbohydrate, 2 g fiber, 5 g protein.

Dough what fun you'll have making these sweet rolls that totally rock!

STICKY RED RASPBERRY ROLLS

Utensils

- Measuring cups
- Measuring spoons
- 2 small saucepans
- 2 wooden spoons
- Hot pads
- Small bowl
- 8×8×2-inch baking pan
- Cutting board
- Sharp knife
- Pastry brush
- Wire cooling rack
- Large plate

Ingredients

Nonstick cooking spray

½ cup seedless red raspberry jam

1 11-ounce package refrigerated French bread dough

2 tablespoons sugar

¼ of an 8-ounce tub reduced-fat cream cheese

1 tablespoon milk Reduced-fat cream cheese, if you like

Fresh raspberries, if you like

Directions

1 Spray baking pan with nonstick spray; save until Step 2. Turn on the oven to 350°. Put jam in a small saucepan. Place on burner. Turn burner to low heat. Stir with a wooden spoon until jam is melted. Turn off burner. Use hot pads to remove from burner. Place on cooling rack. Put 2 tablespoons of the jam in a small bowl. Pour remaining jam into the baking pan.

2 Remove bread dough from package. On the cutting board, use sharp knife to cut dough into 16 slices. Place dough slices on top of the jam in the baking pan. Use pastry brush to brush dough with the jam from the small bowl. Sprinkle tops of the dough slices with sugar.

3 Put pan in oven. Bake 25 to 30 minutes or until rolls are golden brown. Turn off oven. Use hot pads to remove pan from oven. Place pan on cooling rack and cool 1 minute. Place large plate on top of baking pan. Use hot pads to turn plate and pan over so plate is on the bottom. Set on countertop. Carefully lift off pan. Cool slightly.

4 Put cream cheese and milk in another small saucepan. Place on burner. Turn burner to medium-low heat. Stir with a clean wooden spoon until mixture reaches drizzling consistency. Turn off burner. Use hot pads to remove pan from burner. Place on cooling rack Drizzle cream cheese mixture over rolls. If you like, top rolls with additional cream cheese and a raspberry. Serve warm.

Makes 8 servings

Nutrition Facts per serving:
172 calories, 2 g total fat, 4 mg cholesterol, 265 mg sodium, 35 g carbohydrate, 1 g fiber, 4 g protein.

MOVIN' IT

Ready to roll? Then strap on a helmet, get on your bike, and pedal around the block, on the nearest trail, or even up and down your driveway.

91

LOCO HOT COCOA

Utensils

- Measuring cups
- Measuring spoons
- Medium saucepan
- Wooden spoon
- Hot pads
- Wire cooling rack
- 4 mugs
- Small spoon

Ingredients

2	tablespoons sugar
2	tablespoons unsweetened cocoa powder
3	cups fat-free milk
½	teaspoon vanilla
¼	cup buttermints (about 20 mints) Miniature marshmallows or light pressurized whipped dessert topping, if you like

Directions

1 Put sugar and cocoa powder in medium saucepan. Use wooden spoon to stir until mixed. Slowly add milk, stirring until smooth.

2 Put saucepan on burner. Turn burner to medium heat. Heat mixture until warm. Turn off burner. Use hot pads to remove saucepan from heat. Place on cooling rack. Stir in vanilla.

3 Place an equal number of buttermints in each of the 4 mugs. Pour some of the hot cocoa into each mug. Use small spoon to stir cocoa in each mug until mints melt. If you like, top each serving with marshmallows or dessert topping.

Makes 4 servings

Nutrition Facts per serving:
130 calories, 1 g total fat, 4 mg cholesterol, 78 mg sodium, 25 g carbohydrate, 1 g fiber, 7 g protein.

This chocolate concoction will warm you up from the inside out, but remember not to drink it before bed or you'll have crazy dreams.

Robby makes Miley some of his famous
Loco Hot Cocoa before her throat surgery
to help her stop worrying.

INDEX